Community Helpers

Police Officers

by Dee Ready

Reading Consultant:
Donna Shepherd
National Association of Chiefs of Police

Bridgestone Books
an Imprint of Capstone Press

Bridgestone Books are published by Capstone Press
818 North Willow Street, Mankato, Minnesota 56001
Copyright © 1997 by Capstone Press
Printed in the United States of America

Library of Congress Cataloging-in-Publication Data
Ready, Delores.
    Police officers/by Dee Ready
    p. cm.--(Community helpers)
    Includes bibliographical references and index.
    Summary: Explains the clothing, tools, schooling, and work of police officers.
    ISBN 1-56065-513-5
    1. Police--United States--Juvenile literature. [1. Police. 2. Occupations.]
    I. Title. II. Series: Community Helpers (Mankato, Minn.)
HV7922.R43   1997
363.2'0973--dc21

                                96-47732
                                   CIP
                                    AC

Photo credits
Unicorn/Robert Ginn, cover; Eric Berndt, 8; Fred Jordan, 10; Deneve
    Bunde, 12; McDonald, 16; Dennis Thompson, 20
FPG/Mark Scott, 4; Mark Reinstein, 6; Jeffrey Sylvester, 14; Terry Qing, 18

Table of Contents

Police Officers

Police officers keep their communities safe. They protect people and property from criminals. They make sure people obey the law. A police officer's job can be dangerous.

What Police Officers Do

Police officers patrol streets. When someone breaks the law, police officers investigate. This means they find out all they can about what happened. They arrest people who break the law.

What Police Officers Wear

Many police officers wear a uniform. They wear a badge on their shirts. Police officers in uniform usually wear a special hat. Police officers called detectives do not wear uniforms.

Tools Police Officers Use

Police officers carry guns and handcuffs on their belts. In their patrol cars, they use radios to talk to each other. Some use a radar gun to catch people driving too fast.

What Police Officers Drive

Many police officers drive a patrol car. This car has a siren and lights on the roof. Some police officers drive motorcycles or unmarked cars. Unmarked cars do not have lights or markings you can see.

Police Officers and School

Police officers must be at least 18 years old. Some go to college for two years. All police officers study at police academies. Their training can last as long as a year.

Where Police Officers Work

Police officers work at police stations. Some drive around their cities in patrol cars. Other police officers walk around their cities. Some ride bicycles or horses. They make the streets safe for people.

People Who Help Police Officers

Police officers need help, too. A dispatcher at the police station answers emergency calls. Photographers snap pictures of clues. People in the crime lab examine fingerprints, bloodstains, and other clues.

Police Officers Help Others

Police officers help everyone in a community. They protect people from crime. They visit schools to teach kids about drugs and crime. Police officers have very important jobs.

Hands On: Dust for Fingerprints

A police officer sometimes uses fingerprints to find a criminal. Everyone has different fingerprints. When people are arrested, the police fingerprint them. The police keep the fingerprints in a file.

When a crime happens, the police check the crime scene for fingerprints. They try to match them with someone who was arrested.

1. Look for a dark surface someone may have touched. A table might be good.

2. Use a brush to dust the surface with baby powder. The powder will stick to any fingerprints.

3. Find a fingerprint. Tear off a piece of clear tape. Carefully put the tape on the print. Press it down, but do not move it around.

4. Lift the tape up. Stick it on a piece of dark paper. If the print is not clear, try again. Use another piece of tape on the same print. Your first piece probably had too much powder.

Words to Know

community (kuh-MEW-nuh-tee)—a group of people who live in the same area

crime (KRIME)—an action that is against the law

detective (di-TEK-tiv)—a person who tries to solve a serious crime

investigate (in-VESS-tuh-gate)—to ask questions to try to solve a crime

law (LAW)—a rule that helps people live together in peace

Read More

Barrett, Norman S. *Picture World of Police Vehicles*. New York: Franklin Watts, 1991.

Matthis, Catherine. *I Can Be a Police Officer*. Chicago: Children's Press, 1984.

Pellowski, Michael J. *What's It Like to Be a Police Officer?* Mahwah, N.J.: Troll Associates, 1990.

Internet Sites

OnPatrol

http://www.onpatrol.com/

The Police Station

http://www.islandnet.com/~wwlia/police.htm

Index